SPOKEN WORDS

Grief & Despair

M.K. Barreau

Spoken Words: Grief amd Despair

Copyright © 2025 By **M.K. Barreau**

All rights reserved.

Dear readers,

Life's journey is often marked by profound experiences of pain, loss, and grief. These moments, though challenging, shape our souls and reveal the depths of our resilience. In this collection of poems, I delve into the heartache and sorrow that comes with losing loved ones, the anguish of unspoken words, and the heavy silence that grief often brings.

Spoken Words: Grief and Despair is my attempt to connect with you, the reader, through the universal language of pain and healing. I hope my verses resonate with your own struggles and bring solace in knowing that you are not alone.

May these words offer comfort to those who grieve, and may they serve as a reminder that even amid sorrow, there is strength to be found, and love that transcends all.

Welcome to my world of written words!!

With eternal gratitude and love,

M.K. Barreau

Introduction

Here, in these pages, I lay bare the weight of loss, inviting you to journey through its shadows with me. Poetry is my sanctuary—a space where grief takes shape, where sorrow is given voice. This collection is an exploration of absence, longing, and the quiet, consuming nature of despair.

Grief does not move in straight lines. It lingers, shifts, and returns when least expected. Some days, it is numbness; other days, it is an unbearable heaviness. These poems capture that unpredictable journey, embracing the stillness, the confusion, and the search for meaning in what remains.

At the heart of this collection is my grandmother, Anne—my guiding light, even in her absence. She was my strength, my safe place, the foundation of my world. Her presence shaped me, and her absence reshaped me.

This book is dedicated to her memory. To the love that endures beyond loss. To the moments that live on, even when the person is gone. These poems are my tribute, my way of holding on, one word at a time.

Table of Contents

Grief begins in the silence before the storm—
when loss is near but hasn't yet spoken its name.

Twenty-Four to Forty-Eight

The words hit like a storm, "Only 24-48 hours more,"
Reality crystallized, sharper than before.
You are so close to departing this place,
Time, a cruel trickster, quickening its pace.

In these hours, both fleeting and vast,
Moments stretch out, yet rush by so fast.
A day feels eternal, each second a year,
But also too brief, when goodbye draws near.

Not enough time to utter all we feel,
To say "I love you" and make the pain heal.
In one breath, a lifetime, in another, too short,
Emotions tangled in a sorrowful court.

The clock ticks on, relentless and cold,
Each passing minute, a story untold.
We watch the hands move, an agonizing dance,
Caught between despair and a fragile chance.

An hour creeps by, dragging its feet,
While memories flash, bitter and sweet.
The weight of what's coming, heavy and real,
No time to prepare, to process, to heal.

Yet in this expanse of sorrow and dread,
We find fleeting moments, love quietly spread.
A touch of the hand, a comforting glance,
In this endless, brief, heartbreaking dance.

My dear, your journey soon reaches its end,
And we hold on to time, as it tries to transcend.
In these 24-48 hours, eternity and a breath,
We face the inevitable, the closeness of death.

Not enough time, but we hold what we can,
Every second a treasure, in this fleeting span.
Though the clock ticks onward, indifferent and true,
Our love remains timeless, forever with you.

In Limbo's Embrace

In the quiet hush of twilight's veil,
Where time suspends and shadows trail,
A breath, a pause, in limbo's grace,
We linger in this fragile space.

Eyes watch the rise, the fall of chest,
Is this the day she finds her rest?
Each heartbeat whispers, soft and low,
In limbo's arms, we ebb and flow.

A dance between the here and there,
A tethered soul, a whispered prayer,
Not yet to leave, not yet to stay,
We wait and watch, both night and day.

The agony, the silent plea,
To end her pain, to set her free,
Yet selfish hearts, we wish to hold,
Her presence, warm, though frail and cold.

Each moment, precious, bittersweet,
A blessing found in suffering's seat,
We cherish breaths, though shadows creep,
In limbo's watch, we wake and weep.

Is today the day she takes her flight?
Into the stars, beyond the night?
Or will she linger, breathe once more,
On this thin thread, this fragile shore?

In limbo's embrace, we find our way,
Between the dawn and end of day,
In silent vigil, love's pure light,
We hold her close, in darkest night.

Final Slumber

In the stillness of the night's embrace,
I watch her in this quiet space,
Her chest, it rises, gently falls,
In slumber's hold, where silence calls.

Her face, so peaceful, soft and fair,
As if she dreams without a care,
A fleeting moment, I pretend,
She's dreaming dreams that never end.

The truth, I know, lies close at hand,
In this, her final, resting land,
Yet here I sit, my heart in thrall,
To each soft rise, each tender fall.

Her breaths, a whisper, barely there,
A lullaby to soothe despair,
I trace the lines upon her face,
In sleep's serene, forgiving grace.

Oh, let me linger in this lie,
That she's just sleeping, by and by,
That when she wakes, she'll smile again,
And all our grief will reach its end.

But deep within, I feel the sting,
Of time's relentless, cruel swing,
I know what waits, what dawn will bring,
The end of all, this final spring.

Yet for this moment, let me keep,
The vision of her gentle sleep,
Her peaceful dreams, a sweet reprieve,
From all the sorrow, all we grieve.

In sleep, she wanders realms unseen,
In fields of gold, where hearts are clean,
And though I know the end is near,
I hold this vision, crystal clear.

Her final slumber, soft and deep,
In dreams of love, she lies asleep,
And though the dawn will bring the night,
For now, she dreams in purest light.

I Love You Anne

Grandma, I love you, more than words can say,
In this quiet room, where life gently slips away.
I wish to speak, to share what's in my heart,
But silence speaks volumes, even when words depart.

A fleeting glance from you, so tender and wise,
I smile back, love shining in my eyes.
No need for words, we understand,
Our hearts conversing, hand in hand.

Seeing you rest, life's glow slowly fading,
Brings a bittersweet calm, no need for evading.
I smile, knowing soon you'll find your peace,
In a world beyond, where sorrows cease.

Though you'll leave this world, your essence remains,
In the world ahead, free from pain.
A place of life, love, and endless light,
In this thought, I find my solace tonight.

Grandma, your spirit will soar,
In a realm of joy, forevermore.
Though I'll miss you, in this earthly space,
I take comfort in your new embrace.

Rest now, dear Grandma, let go of the strife,
Embrace the love, the eternal life.
In my heart, you'll always stay,
Guiding me, even when you're far away.

Drifting between worlds, where reality blurs and feeling fades—grief numbs before it breaks.

Outer Body

In the room, I sit, an unseen guest,
Watching the tears, the sorrow expressed.
Voices murmur, memories shared,
A surreal tableau, emotions bared.

I drift above, a silent observer,
Detached from my body, my mind a rover.
Faces blurred, yet the grief is clear,
An out-of-body experience, profound and sheer.

I cannot cry, though the pain is near,
Emotionless, while others weep and fear.
This moment feels distant, not part of me,
A dreamlike state, where I cannot see.

Disconnected, as if in a trance,
Watching the scene like a mournful dance.
This isn't real, my mind protests,
A spectator in a film, my heart contests.

I should be crying, but I'm numb inside,
Caught between worlds, where emotions hide.
This isn't happening, I try to declare,
But the sorrow in the room fills the air.

What happens when mind and body reunite?
Will I be overwhelmed by the flood of night?
I fear the moment they intertwine,
Afraid of the grief that will then be mine.

For now, I float, in this surreal state,
A witness to grief, yet emotionally sedate.
What will occur when I come back to me?
I dread the reality I will then see.

So I linger here, in this detached space,
Hoping to avoid the emotional embrace.
An out-of-body experience, strange and profound,
In the midst of sorrow, where tears abound.

Blurred Realities

In sleep's embrace, where shadows play,
I drift through realms of night and day,
A daze enfolds, I lose my way,
What's real, what's not, I cannot say.

Awake, asleep, a seamless dance,
In blurred realities, I glance,
A world surreal, yet so profound,
In waking dreams, I'm ever bound.

I wake to find the dream persists,
In twilight's hold, my mind twists,
Reality, a fleeting ghost,
Of phantoms strange, I am the host.

Is this the day, the light of dawn,
Or night's illusion, curtains drawn?
I wander through this misty maze,
Unsure if I'm in waking haze.

In sleep, I soar on wings of night,
In wake, I drift, in boundless flight,
A paradox, a tangled weave,
In sleep's soft arms, I half believe.

What dreams may come, what visions stay,
In waking hours, they melt away,
Yet linger still, in corners deep,
In restless bounds of fitful sleep.

Am I awake, or lost in dreams?
In this half-light, the boundary seems,
To shift and blur, a whispered breath,
Between life's pulse and dream's soft death.

A question lingers, haunts my mind,
In sleep's embrace, what truth to find?
For in this daze, this twilight's keep,
I wander realms between awake and sleep.

In the Daze of Slumber

In the daze of slumber's grip,
Reality begins to slip,
Awake or dreaming, who can say?
As night blends softly into day.

Eyes wide open, yet I float,
On streams of dreams, a fragile boat,
Waking moments, blurred and thin,
Am I asleep, or am I in?

The world around, surreal and bright,
Merging with the shades of night,
Echoes whisper, shadows play,
In this twilight, lost, I sway.

A fleeting touch, a distant sound,
In waking dreams, I'm spellbound,
Faces, places, drift and gleam,
Which is real, and which the dream?

The line is thin, the veil is sheer,
Between the worlds, both far and near,
I grasp at threads of waking thought,
Only to find them swiftly caught.

In slumber's arms, I'm held so tight,
Yet morning breaks, with piercing light,
Caught between the two extremes,
In waking life and vivid dreams.

A constant dance, a dizzy spin,
Of sleep and wake, of out and in,
Reality, a shifting sea,
Where am I now? Where could I be?

Am I awake, or still asleep?
In waking dreams, my secrets keep,
Surreal worlds, they intertwine,
In this daze, both worlds are mine.

So here I drift, in twilight's gaze,
In waking sleep, in dreaming daze,
Lost in realms where both are true,
In waking dreams, I search for you.

Numb

Feeling something between numb and hysterical,
A pendulum swings, erratic and lyrical.
One moment, a void where nothing resides,
The next, a torrent where the pain never hides.

Numbness creeps in, like a thief in the night,
Stealing my senses, my will to fight.
A cold, empty shell where I can't feel,
Detached from reality, nothing seems real.

Then without warning, the dam breaks apart,
Unstoppable tears flood my aching heart.
Inconsolable cries, a soul laid bare,
Grief overwhelming, too much to bear.

Between numb and hysterical, I teeter on the edge,
A fragile balance, a life on a ledge.
One moment I'm a stone, the next I'm a storm,
A duality within, a heart torn and worn.

Numbness offers solace, a brief reprieve,
A silent whisper, a chance to breathe.
Yet hysteria follows, with a deafening roar,
Reminding me of the pain at my core.

Caught in this cycle, a relentless spin,
Feeling somewhere or something within.
A dance of extremes, a tumultuous tide,
Between stillness and storm, where I can't hide.

In the silence, I yearn for a middle ground,
A place where peace and solace are found.
But for now, I sway in this chaotic flow,
Between hollow and frantic, where emotions grow.

Feeling somewhere or something between numb and hysterical,
A life lived on the cusp, both painful and lyrical.
Navigating the storm, seeking the calm,
In a world where my heart and soul remain drawn.

Drug-Induced

Without any drugs, feeling the effects I didn't take,
Numbness spreads through me, a silent, invisible ache.
Can't feel my head, my arms—am I awake?
My heart? I left it buried in your chest,
The moment the first shovel full of dirt hit your casket.

A haze clouds my mind, emotions turned to stone,
Walking through life, feeling so alone.
Numb to the pain, yet it's there all the same,
A ghostly presence, whispering your name.

Your absence is a drug, potent and cruel,
Leaving me adrift in this endless, empty pool.
I buried my heart with you, deep in the ground,
Lost in the silence where no comfort is found.

The earth swallowed my grief, but it lives in my veins,
Coursing through me like an endless refrain.
Without any drugs, yet feeling their sting,
Lost in the numbness, unable to sing.

I can't feel the world, can't touch or taste,
Living in shadows, a life laid to waste.
My heart is buried, six feet below,
With you, my dear, where flowers don't grow.

The first shovel of dirt, a sound I can't shake,
Sealed my emotions, left in its wake.
Numb to the core, yet hurting so deep,
In the silence of loss, where memories sleep.

Without any drugs, I'm adrift in this pain,
Numb to the touch, yet feeling the strain.
Burying my heart with you, under the earth,
Lost in this void, for all that it's worth.

In the Wake of Your Goodbye

You left me too soon, too fast,
And now I'm adrift, in shadows cast.
I wasn't ready, I still need you here,
I'm lost without you, swallowed in fear.

A void you left, deep in my soul,
Where once was warmth, a heart now cold.
I reach for you, but find empty air,
No guiding light, just a vacant stare.

What am I supposed to do without you?
Where do I go, now that you're through?
You were my compass, my steady ground,
Now I wander, with no path to be found.

I need your wisdom, your gentle hand,
To guide me through this uncharted land.
But you're not here, you've gone away,
And I'm left alone, in disarray.

Please, I beg, don't leave me behind,
I need your strength, your peace of mind.
I'm calling out, though I know you're gone,
In the echoes of night, I carry on.

But it's hard, so hard, without your grace,
I search for you in every place.
A piece of me went with you that day,
And I'm left to stumble, lost in dismay.

So, if you're listening, if you can see,
Send me a sign, some part of thee.
For I need you now, more than before,
To fill this void, this endless sore.

A fragile shift, where reality is questioned, where absence feels unreal, where the mind reaches for something, someone, to make it whole again.

In the Dark of the Night

I lay awake as the hours creep by,
Thoughts running wild beneath the sky.
I know life moves, as it always must,
But you left me here, with shattered trust.

Too soon you're gone, too quick the goodbye,
Now I'm left with questions that multiply.
Unanswered whispers that fill my mind,
Searching for solace I cannot find.

The dark of the night becomes my stage,
A place for sorrow, grief, and rage.
No one beside me, I'm all alone,
Haunted by echoes of the life we'd known.

I reach for you in the silent air,
But all that lingers is despair.
And though the world spins, as it's meant to do,
I'm caught in a moment that's tied to you.

The hours stretch, unyielding, slow,
With nowhere to turn, no place to go.
I'm trapped in this dark, my heart laid bare,
Your absence a weight I can't repair.

Lean On

Who do you lean on when things are hard?
When you're used to relying and leaning on yourself,
When you're the rock for everyone else,
Who becomes the rock for you?

In the quiet hours, the burdens press,
Heavy on your shoulders, a silent distress.
Who do you turn to when the nights grow long,
When you've always been the one standing strong?

Who becomes the rock when your own strength fades?
When you're lost in the shadows, when the light degrades.
Always the pillar, the steadfast, the true,
But who holds you up when the world falls through?

We all need someone to lean on,
A hand to hold when the path feels gone.
Yet here you stand, alone and proud,
Silent in your struggle, not calling out loud.

Who do you lean on when the tears won't cease?
When you need comfort, a moment of peace.
When you've given all, left with an empty cup,
Who is there to help you, to lift you up?

The echoes of your own voice in the dark,
A reminder that you've always been the spark.
But even the brightest flames can wane,
And who will be there to share your pain?

In the heart of the storm, when you're feeling small,
When the weight of the world makes you want to fall,
Who becomes the rock that you can depend,
When you've been the anchor, the unwavering friend?

We all need someone to lean on,
A beacon of hope when hope seems gone.
But in the silence, you stand alone,
Searching for a strength you've never known.

Who do you lean on when things are hard?
When the world feels heavy, leaving you scarred.
You've always been strong for everyone else,
But who will be strong for you, when you need help?

Hold me

In the quiet corners of my soul,
Where shadows whisper secrets untold,
I yearn for a gentle embrace,
In that space where my heart finds its place.

Can you hold me—not in arms, but in knowing,
In the bed of grief where pain is growing?
Hold me in a space both foreign yet near,
A quiet embrace where echoes disappear.

Hold me in the silence, in the depth of the night,
Where tears flow freely, out of sight.
In the void where my spirit cries,
Hold me in the gap where loneliness lies.

Not with hands, but with presence so true,
Hold me in the way that I held you.
In the unseen place, where my soul seeks rest,
Hold me, hold me, and soothe my unrest.

Can you hold me where my dreams have been?
In the space between sorrow and unseen.
Hold me in the void where no one knows,
In the place where my silent need grows.

Oh, hold me in that space, tender and kind,
Where comfort and peace are intertwined.
Hold me, not in a physical way,
But in the space where my heart longs to stay.

Unravel

Always the pillar, steady and tall,
"You're so strong," they say—I carry it all.
Swallowing sorrow, locking it tight,
Hiding my storms behind quiet light.

Who will I lean on when the world grows dark,
When I'm no longer the stoic, silent ark?
Who will stay when my tears finally fall,
When I unravel, who will answer my call?

Who will hold me when I start to break,
When I loosen my grip, let the flood overtake?
When I dare to be open, unguarded, undone,
And finally feel what I've long outrun?

But where do I turn? Who will stand near,
When I am the one who succumbs to fear?
Burdened with strength, yet aching to fall,
Who will catch me—if anyone at all?

Who will I lean on when it's time to break,
To let the sobs come, let the dam quake?
Who will hold me in my moment of need,
When the mask slips off and I'm freed?

Always the rock, always the strong,
Carrying the burden, for so long.
But even the strongest have their time,
To crumble, to shatter, to no longer mime

Who will catch me when I fall apart,
When I peel back the layers, expose my heart?
Who will stand by as I shed my disguise,
And let the tears stream from my eyes?

Who will I lean on when I can no longer hide,
When I let go of all that's bottled inside?
Who will be there when I let myself be,
Vulnerable, open, and finally free?

Sleep fades, the void lingers,
and the weight of absence sinks in.

Avoidance

I avoid the pain, I try, I do,
The ache that follows thoughts of you.
The minute it rises, too sharp, too raw,
I turn away from the grief I saw.

I lose myself in a glowing screen,
Scroll through lives that feel unseen.
A movie plays, a project calls,
Distractions building fragile walls.

Each moment, a shield from what's inside,
The truth I can't face, the tears I hide.
Because when I think, the hurt runs deep,
A wound reopened, a cut that weeps.

So I shift my focus, I change my view,
Anything to not think of you.
But in the quiet, it finds its way,
The pain I've avoided still wants to stay.

I run, I hide, yet it lingers near,
A shadow born of love and fear.
For in avoiding, I only delay
The grief that will come, some other day.

Perhaps one day, I'll face it whole,
This hollow ache that burdens my soul.
But for now, I drift, I stray, I feign,
Doing all I can to avoid the pain.

Sleepless Since You've Gone

I can't sleep since you've been gone,
The nights stretch endless, far too long.
I lay in bed, my mind a storm,
Begging for sleep to take a form.

I toss, I turn, the hours crawl,
Each shadow on the wall recalls
The void you've left, a deep abyss,
A haunting ache, a love I miss.

As if your final slumber woke
A restless grief I can't revoke.
I pray for rest, for peace, for dreams,
But silence answers, torn at the seams.

My mind in turmoil, thoughts collide,
No refuge found, no place to hide.
I wait, I watch, the clock turns slow,
Until exhaustion takes its toll.

And when my eyelids start to fall,
I wonder if you hear my call.
For in this haze of night's despair,
I feel you linger, everywhere.

Wide Awake

I can't sleep since you've been gone,
Each night a battle until the dawn.
Eyes wide open, heart torn in two,
My mind races, always back to you.

This cycle traps me, sleep then wake,
Fragile moments that endlessly break.
Thoughts of you, like waves, collide,
An aching tide I cannot hide.

The dark is heavy, the silence loud,
Memories linger like a shadowed shroud.
I lie there, still, but my heart won't mend,
Breaking anew as the nights extend.

Do you feel this, wherever you are?
Or am I alone beneath this star?
Time may heal, but for now, it seems,
You haunt my nights, you steal my dreams.

Each hour stretches, a cruel refrain,
The clock ticks softly, echoing pain.
I wonder if sleep will ever take
This shattered soul, wide awake.

Stuck in the Loop

I force myself to rise each day,
To shower, to dress, to keep decay at bay.
But every motion feels so small,
Pointless steps in a world that's stalled.

No shower for days, if I have my way,
The effort's too much, too heavy to stay.
The couch becomes my only throne,
In this quiet space, I'm utterly alone.

Too lazy to cook, too tired to move,
The world spins on, but I can't improve.
Sleep comes in shards, day becomes night,
Awake in the dark, avoiding the light.

The TV flickers, a numbing glow,
A hollow escape from the pain I know.
Nothing excites me, nothing feels real,
Not since you left, not since I can't heal.

I'm stuck in a loop, a rhythm of despair,
Going through motions, but I'm not there.
If I could find you, if I could rewind,
Perhaps I'd escape this prison of mind.

But for now, I linger, caught in this fight,
Wrestling shadows, avoiding the light.
Hoping someday, the weight will lift,
And life might feel like more than this drift.

The Void

Depression hit, a silent storm,
An empty ache, a formless form.
No one to talk to, no one to call,
Not like we used to—no, not at all.

Friends and family gather near,
Their love is kind, their words sincere.
But the void remains, so vast, so still,
A hollow space only you could fill.

No one to pray as I start my day,
No quiet words to light my way.
No calls to check if I'm okay,
The world feels colder since you've gone away.

I smile, I nod, I carry through,
But nothing feels as bright, as true.
A shadow lingers, a heavy cost,
The weight of you, forever lost.

Yet here I stand, though cracked and torn,
Facing nights that feel forlorn.
Hoping someday, this pain will cease,
And in its place, a tender peace.

I Miss You

I've missed you since the day you left,
An ache that time has not bereft.
I wish I could hug you, hold you near,
Feel your warmth, dispel this fear.

I miss your smile, so bright, so kind,
The way you'd soothe my troubled mind.
"I love you, baby, mwah," you'd say,
Your voice, my comfort, night and day.

I reach for the phone, my fingers trace,
But you're not there, just empty space.
No more calls, no laughter shared,
A silence that leaves my heart ensnared.

Oh, how I miss you, it cuts so deep,
A longing that lingers, wakes, and sleeps.
If only one more time, we could be,
In each other's arms, just you and me.

But now, you're gone, beyond my grasp,
Yet in my heart, I hold you fast.
I miss you with every breath,
And carry your love beyond your death.

Longing for what can never return...

Can I Go Back in Time?

Can I just go back in time,
To when your laughter matched mine?
To a place where your presence was near,
Where the world felt whole, and you were here.

If only to hear your voice once more,
To see you walk through that familiar door.
To hold you close, to feel your embrace,
To see the light dance upon your face.

I'd build a time machine, no matter the cost,
To recover moments I thought weren't lost.
To turn back the clock, to rewrite the pain,
Just to have you with me again.

Yet you're gone, and I'm left here alone,
Chasing moments that I can't call my own.
I dream of the days when you were near,
And wish for the joy that has disappeared.

Can I go back? Just one more chance,
To relive your smile, your gentle glance.
But the past stays locked, a fleeting scene,
And I'm left yearning for what has been.

Voicemail

I press play to hear you again,
A voice etched in time, a fleeting friend.
A painful comfort, a bittersweet sound,
Your words now echo, where silence is found.

Each message, a nudge, a tug on my heart,
A reminder of all that's been torn apart.
I hold my breath as the seconds fade,
Listening close to the memories made.

Your laughter lingers, your words still warm,
But they can't shield me from this storm.
For when it ends, I'm left to face
The hollow ache of your empty space.

No new hellos, no goodbyes to give,
Just fragments of you, in these moments I relive.
A voice I cherish, though it breaks me in two,
For it whispers the truth—I won't hear more from you.

Yet still, I press play, again and again,
For just a small moment, I feel you within.
And though it hurts, I can't let go,
Your voice, my solace, in the quiet I know

A Vision in Song

In the quiet of the church, I sat alone,
Tears in my eyes, heart like a stone.
The notes of "Ave Maria" filled the air,
And for a moment, I felt you there.

I glanced at the wall, just a fleeting look,
But what I saw made my spirit shook.
Your face, so familiar, came into view,
I blinked, unsure if it could be true.

Was it just a trick of light and tears?
A hopeful dream to calm my fears?
I pulled down my shades, wiped my eyes,
But there you were, to my surprise.

As the song reached its highest note,
I saw your smile, felt it float—
Across the space, so pure, so kind,
Easing the ache within my mind.

I stared at the wall, couldn't look away,
Your image clearer with each sway.
And in that smile, I found my peace,
A gentle warmth, my doubts released.

Maybe it was just my heart's desire,
But in that moment, in that choir,
I knew, somehow, you were okay,
That love transcends what time can fray.

So I smiled back, let the tears flow,
Knowing now what I needed to know.
You're with me still, in heart and grace,
Forever there, in that sacred place.

Echoes of You

I miss your cooking, that comforting taste,
Yet the flavors now blur, like dreams laid to waste.
Have I truly forgotten, or is it the fear
That remembering you means the absence is near?

If I let myself linger on spices and scents,
Will the ache of your absence grow sharper, more dense?
I miss my prayer warrior, steadfast and strong,
The one with enough faith to carry us all along.

How you'd scold me for dresses that danced on my thigh,
With a love that was gentle, a twinkle in your eye.
You'd hold onto my arm, though the world weighed you down,
Your warmth was a fortress, a soft, sacred crown.

I miss the stories of family and lore,
Each tale woven tightly, a rich, vibrant core.
Yet the details slip away, like whispers in air,
I just loved the sound of your voice, always there.

I miss you a lot, more than words can convey,
In the quiet of the night, where your memory stays.
But I fear if I linger too long in the past,
The truth of your absence will grip me at last.

So I hold onto fragments, the laughter, the light,
The warmth of your spirit that still feels so bright.
Though I can't taste your cooking or recall every word,
Your love is a melody, a song still heard.

And in every heartbeat, in each tear that I shed,
You're the light in my darkness, the love I still tread.
I miss you profoundly, and that's okay too,
For in missing you, I'm still close to you.

Grief is not a straight path—it twists,
doubles back, skips steps, and circles around.
You may leave a stage behind, only
to find it waiting for you later.

Reaching for You

I drive these streets we once knew well,
Passing by the places where memories dwell.
I reach for my phone, a habit so true,
Ready to call, just to talk to you.

But then it hits, like a sudden blow,
You're not here, and I already know—
No ringing tone, no voice so dear,
Just silence now, it's all I hear.

I miss the way you'd tease me back,
Your laughter echoing through the cracks.
The way your smile could light the day,
How your love would chase the dark away.

But today, I drive in quiet pain,
Wishing I could hear your voice again.
To tell you I love you, just one more time,
To feel that warmth, so pure, so kind.

I miss you more than words can say,
In every moment, in every way.
But all I have now are memories to hold,
In a world that's grown a little more cold.

So I keep on driving, lost in thought,
Holding tight to the love you brought.
Wishing somehow, you were still near,
That I could call you and you'd be here.

Passing By

It's been months now since you've gone away,
And still, I find reasons to delay.
I come into town, but don't stay long,
The road pulls me forward, keeps me moving on.

There's an exit I know I should take,
A turn I should make for my own heart's sake.
But I speed right past, I look straight ahead,
Running from the truth I haven't yet said.

I should visit your grave, I should see your name,
But the thought of it all feels too much the same—
Like admitting you're gone, accepting it's true,
That this world keeps turning without you.

Maybe I'm not ready to face the stone,
To see the letters etched there alone.
To see the reality carved so deep,
That the silence there is yours to keep.

So, I rush out of town as quickly as I came,
Avoiding the place that bears your name.
It's easier to drive, to keep moving fast,
Than to pull over and face the past.

I tell myself, "Maybe next time I'll go,"
But deep down, I think that I already know—
I'm scared of the moment it all becomes real,
Of standing before what I don't want to feel.

So, I keep on driving, I pass by the way,
But your memory lingers, it doesn't obey.
I carry it with me, wherever I roam,
Though I've yet to visit the place you call home.

One day, I'll stop, I'll let myself cry,
I'll face the truth I've kept passing by.
But for now, I speed on, I just can't yet see
The stone that makes it final for me.

Endless Cycle

I take a step, but then I stall,
Her voice still echoes through it all.
In dreams, I see her smile so clear,
Then wake to find she's nowhere near.

Joy comes softly, I let it stay,
But sorrow slips in anyway.
One moment, light breaks through the gray,
The next, I'm lost, I'm swept away.

I've tried to move, to walk ahead,
But here I stand, where tears are shed.
One day I laugh, the world is bright,
The next, I'm crying through the night.

She left her mark, she carved so deep,
The love that time still aches to keep.
I hold her close, I let her go,
But grief returns, as rivers flow.

It's a cycle, spinning round and round,
The peace is fleeting when it's found.
I find the strength, I lose it, too,
For every joy, there's pain to chew.

Her absence fills each breath I take,
The wounds that heal, then quickly break.
A dance of mourning, joy, and tears,
Of letting go, yet drawing near.

I walk in circles, day by day,
Lost in the things I cannot say.
I move on, yet I stay behind,

Chained by the love she left entwined.
So I surrender, I let it be,
The cycle's grip won't set me free.
I carry on, though I don't know how,
Living in both then and now.

Dreams That Won't Come

I close my eyes and wait for night,
For just a glimpse, for one small light.
She's come to others, smiled and stayed,
But in my dreams, she's yet to wade.

I thought our bond was strong and true,
That love like ours would carry through.
But here I am, night after night,
Left reaching out to empty light.

Was I wrong? Did I not see
The depth of love she had for me?
Or is it something I don't know,
Some secret path I cannot go?

I long to see her face once more,
To find her waiting at my door.
To hear her voice, to feel her near,
To feel the peace I need to hear.

I wait for signs, I strain to hear,
But all that answers is the fear.
Does she wander in a place I can't find,
Or is she resting, leaving me behind?

I tell myself she's safe and free,
That she's at peace, she's finally free.
But oh, how I wish for just one night,
For her to visit and make it right.

To hold her hand, to hear her speak,
To feel the comfort that I seek.
To know what my heart already knows,
That she's at peace, where love still grows.

So I'll keep waiting, though dreams delay,
For the night she finally comes my way.
I'll close my eyes and hope she'll be,
Standing there, at last, with me.

Am I Enough?

Dearest, can you hear me now,
As I question if I've made you proud
I'm striving, I'm trying to follow your way,
But fear whispers I may have gone astray.

I think of you often, your gentle grace,
The kindness that lit up every space.
Your heart so big, your love so pure,
I want to be like you, I want to be sure.

But what if I'm falling short somehow?
Is that why you haven't come to me now?
In dreams, I wait, but you don't appear—
Am I not enough? Is that why you're not here?

I long to know if you're watching me,
If you're proud of the person I try to be.
I stumble, I falter, I question my way,
But I carry your love with me each day.

Please tell me, dear, if you can hear,
Am I doing enough to keep you near?
Am I walking the path you'd choose for me,
Or am I blind to what you'd want to see?

I hold onto memories, I cling to your light,
But shadows of doubt haunt me at night.
I'm doing my best, but is it enough,
To honor your spirit, to mirror your love?

I wish you could tell me, whisper it clear,
That I'm making you proud, that you're still near.
But until you come, until you show,
I'll keep on striving, though I may never know.

For now, I'll follow where your kindness leads,
Planting your love like scattered seeds.
Hoping one day, when I close my eyes,
I'll see your smile and realize—
That I was always enough in your eyes.

Behind the Smile

I try to move on, to let it all fade,
But the tears come back like a tidal wave.
I fight them off, I swallow them down,
Yet still, they rise, and I start to drown.

I want to speak, to let it out,
But I choke on the words, and silence wins out.
My family grieves in their own quiet ways,
And friends have grown weary of what I say.

So, I keep it hidden, buried deep,
The sorrow that steals into my sleep.
I dare not tell a stranger why,
My tears fall heavy when I try.

Tears are a weakness, or so I've been told,
A sign that I'm breaking, that I'm losing hold.
But do the rules change when mourning's involved?
Or must I stay strong until it's resolved?

So, I fight them back, these waves of pain,
I put on a smile, though it feels in vain.
I carry on, day after day,
Pretending I'm fine in every way.

But beneath the surface, where no one can see,
The tears still gather, they wait to break free.
I wish I could share, but I just don't know how,
So, I carry my grief in silence for now.

I hide it well, I wear it like a mask,
Braving each moment, it's all I can ask.
And though I stumble, though I fall apart,
I keep on moving, with tears in my heart.

Acceptance is not forgetting—it's carrying love forward, finding healing in remembrance, and making peace with the absence while still holding on to what remains.

Caught In Between

In the quiet corners of my mind,
I wander paths where memories unwind.
Caught between denial and acceptance's sway,
I grapple with grief, lost in disarray.

To accept feels like letting go,
A distant future where I won't know
Your laughter, your stories, your gentle embrace—
The thought leaves a hollow, an empty space.

Does acceptance mean I've moved on,
That your presence fades, like dew at dawn?
I don't want to forget, to let you slip free,
For you're woven in all that is still me.

I try to pretend this isn't real,
Wrap myself tight in the pain I conceal.
Yet in those moments, stark and clear,
A whisper of doubt brings forth the fear.

Am I still in denial, lost in the night?
Or is acceptance a flicker, a dim, distant light?
I thought I was ready to face the new day,
But it seems that I'm still searching for a way.

To carry your essence, to hold you near,
To honor our bond, to keep you here.
So in this space, where I softly tread,
I'll cherish your memory, though I'm filled with dread.

For acceptance, I know, will come in its time,
But right now, I'm wrapped in this heart's quiet rhyme.
I'm not ready to move on, to say my goodbye,
For in every heartbeat, you're still by my side.

Fading Echoes

I'm so scared, can you hear my plea?
There's so much left unsaid, so much left to be.
I ache with the weight of all I didn't do,
In the silence, I tremble, longing for you.

Is my memory of you already starting to fade?
The colors of moments, once bright, now delayed.
I didn't pay attention, lost in the day,
And now the simplest details slip quietly away.

What did you smell like—sweet lavender's grace?
Or perhaps it was warmth, a familiar embrace?
I strain to recall, but the echoes grow dim,
Your voice, a soft whisper, like a delicate hymn.

What did your hands feel like, so gentle and strong?
The touch that brought comfort, where I felt I belonged.
I don't want to lose you, not now, not again,
Each memory fading feels like a deep, hollow pain.

I hold onto fragments, afraid they will slip,
The laughter, the stories, the warmth of your grip.
In the quiet of night, I reach through the dark,
Clinging to shadows, to each tender spark.

So I'll keep you with me, in every heartbeat,
In the lessons you taught me, in the love that's complete.
Though time may take moments, and distance may grow,
You're woven in my spirit, in the love that I know.

I'm so scared, but I won't let you go,
I'll treasure each memory, let your light always glow.
For in every tear shed, in every sigh,
You're forever my guide, in the whispers of the sky.

Acceptance

Is this it? The final stage,
Where time and sorrow share a page?
Has realization come to call,
Or am I still bound by denial's thrall?

I wear a mask, a painted smile,
Pretending I've accepted all the while.
Yet deep in shadows, where silence reigns,
Your memory lingers, entwined with my pains.

To the outside world, I've moved along,
But in the stillness, I hear our song.
Fighting back thoughts that won't release,
Chasing the echoes, seeking some peace.

The night grows heavy with whispers of you,
And I wonder if acceptance means starting anew.
Or is it a journey through layers of grief,
A slow unraveling, a search for relief?

Each tear a testament, each sigh a plea,
For the love that remains, though you're not with me.
Yet perhaps in this struggle, there's a thread of light,
A path toward healing, softening the night.

So I sit with the pain, let it flow through,
Embracing the memories, holding on too.
For acceptance isn't erasing the past,
It's learning to carry your love, unsurpassed.

In the quiet, I breathe, I allow,
To feel every moment, to honor the now.
And though you are gone, in my heart you reside,
In accepting my loss, I learn to abide.

The Tangle of Grief

Denial, anger, bargaining, grief,
All came at once, like a thief,
Unraveled moments, they swirl and collide,
A tempest of feelings I cannot abide.

These stages aren't linear, they twist and they turn,
Unpredictable currents, a fire that won't burn.
Am I grieving wrong if I miss out on parts?
Is there a right way to mend broken hearts?

What does grief look like? I search for a sign,
In the quiet of the night, in the spaces divine.
Is it tears that fall freely, or silence that weighs?
Is it laughter that echoes through memory's haze?

I can't make sense of this tangled refrain,
Each feeling a puzzle, a dance with the pain.
Am I grieving at all, or just lost in the haze,
In a fog of confusion, where time seems to blaze?

I've held on to fragments, both heavy and light,
Carried the burden, embraced the night.
In moments of stillness, I feel you near,
Yet doubt creeps in, whispering fear.

But maybe grief isn't a path to be tracked,
Maybe it flows in waves, gently stacked.
A tapestry woven of joy and of sorrow,
A journey unfolding with no clear tomorrow.

So I'll honor the chaos, the mess and the ache,
For in this wild dance, I'm learning to take
Each moment as it comes, a breath, a release,
Finding my way toward a fragile peace.

In the heart of the storm, I'll learn to be brave,
Embracing my journey, the love that I crave.
For grief has no rules, no single display,
It's a portrait of love in its own, tender way.

Reflection is a bridge to the past, where nostalgia weaves memories into echoes. Their absence is heavy, yet their legacy lingers in the spaces they once filled.

Birthday Wishes

On this day, the candles flicker low,
A birthday whispers through the silent glow.
Once, her voice would dance upon the air,
Warm wishes wrapped in love, beyond compare.

But today the phone stays still, no call,
Just echoes of laughter that used to fill the hall.
Her gentle chuckle, a melody divine,
Now just a shadow, a heart's fragile line.

Each moment drags, a weight on my chest,
In the quiet, I feel the ache manifest.
This first year without her, the void feels vast,
A bittersweet reminder of a love that's passed.

How I long for the softness of her words,
The way she'd paint my dreams with hopes like birds.
Each "Happy Birthday," a treasured embrace,
Now only silence fills this empty space.

Oh, to hear her voice just once more,
To hold her in memory, to cherish, to store.
But I carry her with me, though miles apart,
In every beat of my ever-heavy heart.

So I light the candles, close my eyes tight,
And whisper her name in the soft, fading light.
Though she's not here, her love still remains,
In the quiet of my heart, through all the pains.

A Lifelong Journey

I'm happy thinking, feeling, and knowing,
That you're in a better place, where love is glowing.
Yet I don't believe my grief will ever cease,
And truthfully, I don't want it to ease.

Each tear is a tether, each sigh a sweet thread,
Connecting me to all the words left unsaid.
Grief is a journey, a winding, long road,
Not marked by the end, but by love's heavy load.

While I can rest easy, knowing you're at peace,
I embrace this journey, let the sorrow release.
For in every memory, in laughter and light,
You're woven through moments that dance in the night.

And I hold on to hope, a bright, shining star,
That if I live right, though we're worlds apart,
One day we'll meet again, in a place full of grace,
Where love knows no bounds, and time has no trace.

So until then, dear one, rest in your light,
I'll carry your spirit, through days dark and bright.
With every heartbeat, I'll honor your name,
For love is eternal, and we're never the same.

In the quiet of night, when I whisper your song,
I know that you're with me, where I truly belong.
So I'll walk this path, with you ever near,
In the tapestry of love, I'll hold you dear.

Well Done

Grandma, your journey has reached its end,
A life well-lived, my dearest friend.
As you approach those pearly gates,
In heaven's arms, eternity awaits.

God looks down, a smile so bright,
"Well done," He says, in the heavenly light.
Your prayers, your songs, your praise so true,
None of it was in vain, all seen through.

You lived each day with love and grace,
A beacon of faith, in this earthly place.
Now walk the streets of gold so pure,
In God's embrace, forever secure.

"Welcome home, my child," He calls,
As heaven's glory around you falls.
Arms open wide, a loving embrace,
You find your peace in this holy space.

When this life ends, we seek that eternal light,
To hear those words, in the sacred night.
"Well done," the sweetest song,
In God's kingdom, where we belong.

Your singing, your prayers, all rewarded now,
A crown of life upon your brow.
You lived well, in every way,
And now in paradise, you'll forever stay.

Grandma, your faith, your love, your strife,
All led to this, your eternal life.
In heaven's glow, where angels sing,
You're home at last, under God's wing.

So walk through those gates, streets of gold,
In heaven's beauty, your story told.
Your journey complete, your spirit free,
In the arms of the Lord, for eternity.

Gran Fanm (Grand Dame)

Gran famn, our grand dame true,
With grace that time could not subdue,
A presence strong, yet gentle, kind,
A beacon for each heart and mind.

In every word, in every deed,
She sowed the seeds of love and need,
A guiding light, a steadfast flame,
Gran famn, she lived up to her name.

Her wisdom, vast as ocean's span,
Her laughter, bright as morning's plan,
In every story, touch, and smile,
She made our lives more worthwhile.

A grand dame, regal, poised, and fair,
With strength and courage, rare and rare,
In her embrace, we found our home,
With Gran famn, we'd never roam.

Through trials, storms, and life's demands,
She held us with unwavering hands,
A matriarch, both fierce and sweet,
With her, our lives were made complete.

Her legacy, a timeless thread,
In every tear, in words unsaid,
Her spirit lingers, ever near,
Gran famn, our hearts will hold you dear.

In dreams, in whispers, soft and low,
Her presence guides us as we go,
A grand dame's love, forever stays,
In memories and cherished days.

Gran famn, you are our star,
A guiding light, no matter how far,
In every heart, your name will reign,
Our grand dame, forever the same.

Your Legacy

What you leave behind, dear heart,
Nothing in this world can match,
A legacy so finely crafted,
By your hands, with love, unmatched.

Your strength and determination,
Paved the way for all of us,
We wouldn't be where we are,
Without your guiding, steadfast trust.

Oh, what is a legacy,
But the impact that you've made,
A long-lasting, bright reflection,
In the paths your life has laid.

From your faith, so deeply rooted,
To your values, strong and true,
You've instilled in us a purpose,
That will guide us, ever new.

You saw a brighter future,
And created it with care,
For us to thrive and flourish,
With your vision always there.

For that, we thank you deeply,
For the life you chose to lead,
An example, pure and radiant,
In every word, in every deed.

You are and always will be,
A light that guides our way,
In the hearts of generations,
Your legacy will stay.

Matriarch

In the garden of my life, a rose blooms bright,
Her petals spread wide, a radiant glow of light.
Matriarch, leader, with hands soft yet strong,
She weaves through my days, a nurturing song.

With wisdom and grace, she paved every road,
In her footsteps, I've walked, my burdens she showed.
Her strength, a foundation, upon which I stand,
Her sacrifices, countless, like grains of sand.

In her arms, I found solace, in her smile, a home,
Through trials and triumphs, I was never alone.
More than a grandmother, a pillar, a guide,
In her love and support, I've always confided.

Her stories, a tapestry, woven with care,
A legacy of courage, beyond compare.
Without her, I'd falter, lost in the night,
She is my compass, my northern light.

To call her just "grandmother" feels far too small,
For she is the reason I am here at all.
A matriarch, a role model, a beacon so clear,
Without her, I would not be here.

Her essence, a blessing, her spirit, a flame,
Her love, a guiding light, forever the same.
In her embrace, I find strength and pride,
My grandmother, my hero, forever by my side.

*To have loved, to have known, to have shared even
a fleeting moment—what a quiet, sacred gift.*

Loss does not erase the fortune of having had.

About the Author

M.K. Barreau is a poet and writer who channels her deepest emotions into the written word. With *Spoken Words: Grief amd Despair*, she offers a window into her soul, laying bare the intricacies of her experiences with loss and grief. For Barreau, words are more than just language—they are a medium through which she transforms pain into poetry, creating a bridge between her inner world and the outer reality. Through her raw and evocative writing, she brings a voice to the complexities of human emotion, offering solace and understanding for those navigating their own journeys through loss.